Elegy

The University of Alberta Press

Photographs by YUKIKO ONLEY

E.D. BLODGETT

Elegy

Only ghosts will cross
the landscapes that compose
the soul

until my soul
becomes
a ghost

Wherever you are
I give you the rain
to wash your body

wherever you are
I give you the sun
to dry your bones

wherever you are
I give you the moon
to lift you from the earth

wherever you are
I give you the tears of children
to carry you out to sea

Once I saw your breath
suspended in the air

then I understood
how fire could be white

when I exhaled   my breath
followed yours into

the sky that holds us both

Moon   sea   tide
none of them can be borne
coming and going in their

eternal circle of
unremitting solace

I want the barest of rocks
that through millennia of rain
are sand   dust   void

You used to pause beside
a tree a rock a lake
to see it as it was

and when you saw it   you
transferred it into line
a piece of sky and ground

and they look back at you
alone upon the space
that you have given them

nothing stays but these
lines defining space
the only traces these

absence is all that you
have given me to mark
the pauses you have made

I thought of making you
a shrine and on it I
would place a feather and

the bones of mice that I
had found beside a road
and near the top there will

be nothing more than breath
the breath of trees when all
the light of day is gone

the shrine will rest where you
have gone upon the waters
of the world alone

I thought of doing this
and there within my thoughts
it rests   the water where

it floats the water that
becomes the rain that pours
forever through my mind

How beautiful they are
the faces of children in
the sun so full of fire

they form a cosmos of
their own where each of them
illuminates the air

each of them a star
inviolate and filled
with their eternity

the only face I want
is yours and just as death
took it empty away

the one eternity
of my desire where
water flows slowly

toward the sea where all
the light that you possessed
goes out upon the tides

Music rose up and filled
my window with its sound
coming into the room

if music could be torn
apart   I would break
it into silent shards

and throw it back into
the air as if it had
become a small field

of stones that I had tossed
across the world to fill
it with an absence of

the least joy that would
remove from me the light
that lifted from your eyes

when darkness came upon
them and the silence of
your dying filled my ears

Just as when you lived
you lie inside my heart
and now when you are dead

you have no other place
to lie but here inside
the grave my heart became

If the place where you
lay down and died is but
water flowing away

what is my heart that looked
at you as air and fire
leaping through the world

what is my heart but now
composed of water and
its surge of emptiness

Someone brought a rose
and when she left I took
the petals from the stem

one by one and threw
them from the window where
they hung a moment in the air

the wind scattered them all
across the street and grass
so none could tell if they

had fallen from the same
flower and all they were
were petals from nowhere here

this will be enough
the one memorial
that I can think to give

I never wished to have
a rose or any gift
to bring you back to mind

where you are what I think
and what calls out to me
through water tides and rain

give me water to hold
where I can take you in
flowing over my flesh

there eternity moves
on me and in it you
in your moving are held

I have put fire
away and light and air
give me but the rain

that falls across the world
upon the sea and on
the rivers streams and creeks

then there cannot be
anything that I
would want beyond the water

that you have now become
the sea that flows around
the earth and all the lakes

and let the rain take
me wherever it might fall
and then together we

will wash the smaller reeds
that stand upon the shores
grateful for all that falls

What is memory but
fragments of things as they
come randomly to mind

things that are not seen
as if revealed from every side
but just an aspect caught

obliquely passing by
when taken by surprise
by unexpected sounds

all that is recalled
is all that can be gleaned
as light glancing off

another light before
its going out against
the dark where nothing waits

petals of roses fall
into the mind so
and just the slightest breeze

brings them near enough
to touch almost before
they go and you are left

uncertain whether it
had been a rose or what
you thought had been a rose

People were coming out
of church their faces full
of music prayer and peace

why do I look for you
among faces that are
unmoved by signs of grief

if I were going to look
for any face of yours
I might find it in

the shade that trees with small
leaves have cast against
a wall when breezes move

through them from time to time
it seems to be a stream
the wind has riffled in

the sun where patches of
the sun lightly dance
across it as it makes

its way among the fields
and past the sleepy cows
the long lines of trees

o what a fool I am
to think the water that
contains your body is

so pastoral as if
any movement were
enough to carry you

if you can hear me when
I cry out to you
please forgive this wish

that in your death there be
an end to chaos and
tranquillity had come

One of your letters lay
open beside me
on a table as if

forgotten and then found
again because the light
of afternoon had changed

or was it I who was
suddenly open then
who had not seen what you

had said of you and me
of what you too forgot
and then recalled surprised

I want to write to you
and ask you why you do
not die and ask you then

why there is nowhere I
can send what I might ask
before forgetting you

Your drawings hurt most
because they are so mute
without the sound of words

that echo words that you
have read of poets in
their grief and long laments

no words of mine appear
among the drawings on
your page but yours and theirs

why is sorrow just
what poets say when grief
cuts deeper than the words

so finely crafted that
grief becomes but
music charm and sighs

your drawings say more
without a touch of sound
without the echoes that

put the mind asleep
and take from it the stab
of death that comes and stays

Some of the objects in
the room are things we knew
but when you are not here

what will they signify
unable to return the light
becoming mere things

On certain days a kind
of equilibrium
occurs and when the wind

is blowing steadily from
the east in the morning then
at dusk it turns around

death has no greater grasp
than life and darkness does
not overwhelm the light

these are days that do
not come to me or if
they do   they are not known

as other than the shades
of something in the past
of someone else's life

I take another note
of yours into my hands
to gaze upon the sketch

that holds up the words
its inability
to speak gazing at me

as if it were a child
that had just been born
its tongue unused to seize

the shape of words and so
it merely utters *o*
its mouth taken by

astonishment before
falling mute again
the only answer I

can muster is an *o*
that only I can hear
your sketch unable to

take in the least sound
as children who are deaf
or children but still born

How did I dare to say
that I would be the one
that would forget you

rather I should ask
what do rivers recall
when they go down to sea

so I stare at the sea
and know that I am not
recalled or known or seen

A small object of yours
was placed into my hands
I saw it was a stone

that you would carry in
the hope it would protect
you moving over the earth

I tried to make it warm
but it refused and lay
inertly in my hand

without you to keep
it warm it must be just
a stone and cold and dead

I want your hand in mine
without it I will be
a stone too and cold

You never spoke of God
so where to begin
and will you hear my thoughts

God for me was in
your hands but not so much
when you were sketching but

your hands at rest when you
were gazing into space
then they were the hands

of one abandoned to
the world as it was
without the least defence

why was God there
because I think that God
is everywhere inside

and out and yet he is
constrained in every move
he is and that is all

and we are those who leap
who fall who disappear
and stand in rain to wait

So when at night I say
my prayers who will be there
to hear what I might say

not you not God but just
myself and I have heard
all these murmurs before

that fill the air inside
my room and cling to all
the objects there unsure

of what their purpose is
prayers are only us
and in them we become

someone else who
fills a larger space
with more uncertainty

Why have I failed to speak
of tears that I have shed
tears that have filled the night

and left the waning moon
and all the stars that fill
the sky obscure with grief

why have I failed to speak
of silence that comes upon
me night and day and stands

forever at my side
the one companion you
have left me to know

why have I failed to speak
of my desire to step
into the sea where you

have gone into the dark
ahead of me to show
me where I am to go

O sea speak to me
and tell me gently where
it is that I must go

I fear the darkness of
the water where I must
descend and fear what lies

beneath your great expanse
where ships have gone before
never to return

o sea you are where all
that lies hidden in
my heart lies at rest

and there will be no rest
for me until the grave
that my heart is is his

On certain rainy days
I place flowers in
a bowl to give the rain

some colour perhaps
and bring a little light
into my darkened room

since the day I saw
the image of your face
floating there I have

begun to hesitate
I know that everywhere
that water is that you

are in it   nowhere else
to be   but how can I
be free of you when you

can float like any ghost
upon the sea and now
with flowers in a bowl

I want to stop all this
my longing for the sea
my need to ease the rain

I dreamt that I was not
myself but had become
a young birch that grew

beside a quiet stream
I understood that I had been
reborn   my old life gone

the wind blew gently through
my leaves and when it rained
the rain was simply rain

and as a birch I had
no other dreams than those
of birches root and branch

but when the waters of
the stream entered me
I knew that it was you

and even born again
it seems that I am I
and you are always you

dreams have nothing to do
with who we are and will
remain birth after birth

The words uttered here
are like the words that one
might write on water in

the dark   the letters all
askew and each of them
drowned before a sense

of sense can be made out
and if you were to hear
they would be calls that birds

would make asleep in trees
or echoes of their cries
the words not mine not me

The trees are draped in fog
people say it is
the sea that exhales fog

but standing in it who
can tell if it is I
who breathes or if the sea

I think that it is I
and you from in the sea
who are exhaling toward

each other our breath
together forming fog
in moments when I seem

to leave myself behind
upon a shore and you
perhaps lift off the sea

We are now both ghosts
I have given up
my home and you have left

yours forever behind
and so the only place
we have to share is air

now it is possible
for us to meet but so
invisible we will

not know it when we pass
each other hardly more
substantial than our souls

exhaled   no other way
to reach you in your dark
country alive or dead

You never said if there
were fireflies in that
country where you grew up

as soon as darkness falls
they spring alive to save
the darkness from the dark

if you are not too close
they seem no more than lights
going on and off

around you in the air
like small ships upon
the sea signalling to

each other saying they
are still afloat and that
the darkness holds no fear

this is how the dark
plays lightly with us
making us believe

that light never fails
a make believe for those
who breathe the air alone

I think my heart will break
hearing children laugh
below me in the street

go back go back I want
to cry as if I were
crying to them to leave

and yet it is not their
laughter now that I
have called upon but yours

thinking that when I hear
all that joy it must
be yours that fills my room

how my heart is torn
that I should ask you to
depart already gone

If you are in my heart
why do I think that I
will find you in the sea

if you are in my heart
why do I think that fog
will help me breathe you in

if you are in my heart
what permits me to be
in you while in the light

if you are in my heart
what do I carry there
that has no weight at all

but bears on me as if
my life had suddenly
given birth to stars

The day that stars appeared
to shine inside my soul
I lay upon the ground

afraid and waiting for
what had to be my end
but the end did not arrive

and I stood up unsure
what had befallen me
why me why stars and what

destiny has stopped
in me my body now
a womb entire that waits

upon a universe
questions do not form in me
but time that waits and space

But in the universe
I am no larger than
the merest atom or

if animal then flea
the stars would be too large
for me to comprehend

if prayer is allowed
take from me these stars
that now are burning in

the firmament that is
my soul's only sky
I fear that all my breath

will be consumed in that
fire they are and I
like you will disappear

I am waiting for a tree
not the birch I dreamt
but a tree that has

a canopy as broad
as all the skies that stretch
above my soul and I

shall lie beside its feet
and hope that sleep will come
to me beneath the stars

then I will not be
so naked as before
open to nothing but

the sky and all the light
that fills it pouring down
upon me without shade

I heard my bones begin
to speak slowly to me
it was a murmur so

quiet I thought it was
the sound of trees along
horizons speaking to

each other of the sun
upon their naked bark
of winter and its length

the burden of the sound
not heard but sensed along
the edges of the soul

I have never heard
my bones speaking before
and what they spoke of was

the darkness that was theirs
a darkness that was all
they were and of their fear

of any sudden light
where they might disappear
this darkness is mine

I thought and in it I
can sleep without the need
for trees the sea and fog

Music of bones is all
my soul can bear   the song
they make a song that floats

like leaves upon the blood
coming and going without
a trace   their memory

effaced too soon to know
where they were has gone
music then without

a wake but music that
moves forever through
the dark without the fear

that it has lost its way
music abandoned to
itself and blood and dark

Being is blood   the quick
of it entering
my soul in darkness to

suffuse the space I have
become   impossible
to think my soul to be

other than this slow
cadence that begins
inside the murmur of

my bones until the thought
of emptiness lies down
beside me sleeping in

the movement of my blood
where what I am takes shapes
known only to itself

How can I speak of blood
and think that it is mine
if anything it is

a past not known about
and you who now with all
the things that flow are one

and all that I might be
is in that flow that comes
from where time began

filling me in its
forever going round
and round in mysteries

of tides and moons and shores
nothing then is mine
possessed of such returns

A leaf is nothing else
without the barest sense
of where its life comes from

it hangs upon a branch
in sun and rain and dark
its capability

its being there alone
neither forsaken nor
waiting and being is

all that it can be
nor does it know where it
might be but in the air

its only movement from
the wind   its stillness from
the parting of the wind

I know that solitude
belongs to kings but this
infinitesimal leaf

is not alone and when
autumn comes it falls
its wake invisible

yet traced in the air where it
continues to exist
before reaching the ground

there beneath its tree
it takes its rest   a part
of other leaves that lie

upon the late grass
and when autumn comes
it falls in me   the wake

it makes the way my thought
of it unfolds and when
I sleep   it rests in me

Without my knowing how
I have become grass
and it takes root inside

my soul beneath the stars
which fill my soul's sky
but they remain so far

nearest then is grass
and its fragility
that is in me as I

must be in it   the smell
of its autumnal weight
gently rising in me

if I lie down here
it will be in the fall
of all mortality

Your fall must be there
a fall it seems that we have
taken together through

an unresisting air
our leafiness the life
and death we share as we

descend beneath the stars
it is not water that
leaps up to greet us but

the slower rush of blood
that flows on the ground I am
and through the patient grass

this is now the all
that we can be before
my fall into the dark

What is this silence that
descends upon my soul
as if the void began

to fall through itself
its wake impossible
to hear as if the leaf

I knew had disappeared
into an absolute
absence of everything

this is silence none
can bear and if I cry
what will echo back

to me the words I cry
as if all prayer fell
into the silence where

it rises from without
the barest trace of it
in memory left to hear

The last silence is God
and when he is moved to speak
it must be things that form

the sentences that he
chooses to bring forth
the leaf that falls must be

a word   a part of all
he speaks and air and stars
and so must I if I

becoming a leaf that falls
beneath the distant stars
spring forth from that mouth

unheard upon the ground
gathered in what he says
being exhaling me

its silence filling all
that falls coming to rest
upon the silent earth

Grave simplicities
are all my soul can bear
things that can be known

by touch alone when one
lies naked in the dark
things that do not move

but stand as they have stood
before my fingers were
open upon their smooth

unyielding surfaces
and things that have become
the silence of the world

silence that is a long
embrace where all that has
departed lingers in

its going away and takes
upon itself a shape that can
be grasped if not so known

it can be fully named
even rivers when
they pause   possess a shape

that is unyielding and
familiar in the hand
before falling away

And if rivers then
you can also pause
against fingers that

stretch forth into the dark
but what to know beneath
my hand that has not touched

you ever so smooth and so
unyielding yet detained
briefly before you are

carried away from me
so perhaps a leaf
that falls upon a stream

and seems to fall into
sudden stillness before
it makes its way downstream

gravely you have been
given to my hands
not quite a fallen leaf

but something known and not
so known that is of me
and something else where you

have gone without a word
but what remains remains
as if eternity

had paused for the briefest stay
an aspect of itself
graven on my flesh

What to do with this
that is more than a mark
upon my flesh where it

has fallen gentle as
a leaf but a leaf more
enduring in its trace

I have not asked for this
as I would not have asked
that any eternity

approach so near to me
but now it is too late
and if my hand lay on

the table next to me
a flower would stand up
in it seeking the air

Certain flowers must
only be a gift
but gifts that are to be

given up as one
might give something of
oneself away without

demurral as one is said
to give one's soul to God
and so this flower must

be given to the sea
and with it as a shade
the hand from which it sprang

both to make their way
into the dark to give
themselves wholly away

as my tokens to
what spirits guard the world
obdurate in their wake

My hand has ghosted into
the sea followed by
the flower that had sprung

unbidden on its flesh
the gift that I must give
and as they disappear

I know that you have come
imperceptibly
into my soul where you

take up a residence
beneath the stars that fill
its distant firmament

no gift given without
a giving up to that
dwelling of death we are

The eye that can discern
a tree a bird and grass
is not the eye that knows

that you have entered me
nor do I have the sense
the blind possess when all

that lies in the world lies
at rest inside their hands
nor did astonishment

come over me and leave
me breathless at the change
yet I have seen the leaves

of poplar trees on days
when no one feels the wind
unbelievably

tremble without pause
for that moment I
became a poplar tree

a wind unmoving in
me moving what there was
of me that could be moved

and then it passed and all
was still as if there were
no wind and what I thought

had been a leafy tree
was but another dream
from which I wake up

Invisible the sea
seems to rise in me
not the water but

depths unfathomable
where nothing can be known
impossible to say

who it is I am
given up to this
unspeakable of gifts

that I must be but can
not be now called to bear
what none can bear in flesh

or spirit through the world
and yet to give it up
is the last of all gifts

Cover me gently with
the breath of solitude
that I might lie alone

in my mortality
unnoticed by the sea
the tides   the moon   the stars

the slightest frame of flesh
is all that I can be
unable to become

the falling rain a leaf
or any other trace
of God's exhaling the world

Prayer is no avail
the sea does not withdraw
and all of it unto

its farthest caverns rests
in me unyielding to
the least appeal of mine

it is the sheath that you
to me are borne inside
God surrounding you

in water as it floats
in air and nothing we
possess can alter this

inevitable moon
that now ascends upon
the sea to greet the stars

The movement of the world
is so ceremonious
and grave its passing seems

to leave no wake at all
the being of it is
its turning through itself

and what there is to see
is planets stars and moon
but where they turn is not

in those heavens we see
their turning is in us
and where we live is in

that movement that we are
immeasurable and
beyond our knowing here

I cannot say how long
I have been gazing on
this chair with wonder that

its being here is being in
the turning of the stars
astonished that I thought

the stars so far from me
in heavens that are not
for any to attain

and where the blood that turns
in me is going round
there their turn is

and so tides and so you
are their unmeasured turn
and what there is of me

Whatever is is dance
the merest flower that
unfolds opens in

to dance beneath the sun
this table where I sit
unmoving on the floor

turns forever with
the turning earth and I
with it unable to

resist my being this
turning and turning through
the heavens of the stars

and at the heart of all
that I am capable
of being death unfolds

turning through the tides
where you turn beneath
the moon your solitude

gathered in the heart
that turns in me in turn
through your unfolding death

So my waking turns
to sleep deep as the sea
with all that it has borne

a solitary bird cries out
against the starry sky
its unaccompanied song

music does not fall
from its mouth but only light
falling through the dark

until it falls into
my heart as if it were
its only place to fall

music of light has no
melody known but when
its presence is announced

nothing remains untouched
turning to light within
the dark that silently

withdraws becoming just
the shadow of the dance
its finalities

the gift that gives the soul
its bright necessities
among the floating stars

WRITING A POEM IS A VERY MYSTERIOUS ACTIVITY. Seeing poems unfold into a book is even more mysterious; thus I have generally refrained saying how this occurs in me. Once I prepared some notes to talk about my exchange of poems with Jacques Brault which resulted in our *renga*, but in this instance I could talk about how the exchange came to be, how we agreed to respond to our poems, and what kinds of practices we decided on for the translations. How the poems came to be went without comment.

The origin of *Elegy* differs from those of other books I have been engaged in. There is, in fact, a little story behind it, but its execution still remains a mystery. Before I met Yukiko, it must be said that I did not know Toni Onley personally and barely knew his work. I read of his untimely death in *The Globe and Mail* toward the end of February 2004 and shook my head at the circumstances. He had been practising taking off and landing on the Fraser River. My maternal grandfather was a cigar-smoking painter of landscapes whom I had never seen without at least a tie and a vest. Small planes did not fit with my notion of painting landscapes. But I had much more to learn.

Toward the end of the following month I happened to be in Vancouver to give a lecture and a poetry reading. After the reading a somewhat shy Japanese woman approached me to talk briefly about the reading. She then invited me to her studio the following day for a session of photographs for a series she was doing on artists and writers. I smiled and refused on the ground that I have never felt photogenic. She smiled and insisted, saying there was no such thing as an unphotogenic person. Reluctant but persuaded, I agreed to meet her the following day. It was spring in Vancouver, the car was a convertible, and I began to feel photogenic.

I remember, of course, the flowering trees more than anything else. Anyone coming from Edmonton in the depths of winter would have also been awe-struck.

Just before reaching the studio Yukiko asked if I had ever written poems on commission before, and, as she later confided, this idea came to her spontaneously while driving beneath the beautiful, flowering trees. Carefully, I replied that I had written a hymn or two for the Anglican church where I sing in the choir and also a bawdy lyric for the Queen's Jubilee on the occasion of a celebration of both Elizabeths. Of course I guessed what was about to be proposed, and suddenly I felt lacking in both photogenic qualities and poetic skills. But Yukiko persisted and asked if I would write a poem for Toni. I demurred and said I would give her an answer at the end of the sitting. After an hour of photographs and all the funny exchanges that pass between photographers and their subjects, I slowly said I would, but it probably be a little series, since it took me awhile to know where poems would go. My reward was one of Toni's lovely watercolours.

And so I returned to Edmonton, unsure what I had agreed to. I was teaching at the time and busy as writer-in-residence at Grant MacEwan College, so I decided to let matters take their course. I was also busy with a book of prose poems, so I was fully occupied. Finished at the college, I went to Europe for a couple of weeks and then came home where I saw the painting, remembered the request, looked at what had become an Edmonton spring, and did what poets often do when reckoning with a commission. I continued to look at spring. Then one day I began to write 'only ghosts' and the words that followed. How that poem reached the next poem I cannot say, but I knew that after the first few poems this was not going to be a little series. Something had reached into me that was not going to leave until it was assuaged, and the poems began to come at a rate of three, sometimes four, a day. What's more, I had the feeling they were breaking through my head in their eagerness to see the light. This may seem an odd image: I usually sense a poem coming from the heart and issuing through the mouth, knowing all the while that the mind is present, but present, I suppose, in the heart. In this instance, everything had collapsed: my heart was in my mind along with my mouth. And so they were written with both pain and elation, since I was not entirely sure what was happening. Normally I feel myself to be a vehicle through which the poem moves on its way to the world, but inasmuch as this was happening more rapidly than I usually work, I began to feel continually more helpless. The experience reinforced my notion that I wrote for a muse. In this instance the muse had unexpectedly arrived in Yukiko and was speaking to me through her. Inasmuch as this happens regularly in Homer, I was not surprised. In fact, I rejoiced poetry was still in the same graceful place as it had been centuries ago.

So it should be clear that *habent sua fata libelli*, and one can never be sure how their destinies will come and go. At moments even I felt unsure of where I was speaking from—myself, Yukiko or the muse herself. I see that I have really only elaborated upon a mystery. I am not sure whether there is any other way it can be done. Yet if one is in fact in the possession of a muse in the process of writing a poem, it can be no other way. Muses are, as Hesiod reminds us, the daughters of memory, remembering for us what we need to remember, and how we need to remember. This is why the book owes so much to Yukiko, who brought me into necessary memory. Why have I called it simply *Elegy*? If I know Yukiko's sorrow in any way, I know it as the sorrow of loss that everyone knows. And knowing it, I know it as elegy, in which sorrow is transmuted. Once transmuted, it is hers and mine and everyone's.

E.D.B.

Published by
The University of Alberta Press
Ring House 2
Edmonton, Alberta, Canada   T6G 2E1

Text copyright © 2005 E.D. Blodgett
Photographs copyright © 2005 Yukiko Onley

LIBRARY AND ARCHIVES CANADA
CATALOGUING IN PUBLICATION

Blodgett, E.D. (Edward Dickinson), 1935–
Elegy / E.D. Blodgett ; Yukiko Onley, photographer.

ISBN 0–88864–450–7

    1. Grief—Poetry. I. Onley, Yukiko, 1949–
II. Title.
PS8553.L56E44 2005   C811'.54   C2005-904088-2

All rights reserved.
First edition, first printing, 2005.
Printed and bound in Canada by Houghton Boston
Printers, Saskatoon, Saskatchewan.

A volume in (currents), a Canadian literature
series. Jonathan Hart, series editor.

No part of this publication may be produced, stored
in a retrieval system, or transmitted in any forms or
by any means, electronic, mechanical, photocopy-
ing, recording, or otherwise, without the prior
written consent of the copyright owner or a licence
from The Canadian Copyright LicensingAgency
(Access Copyright). For an Access Copyright license,
visit www.accesscopyright.ca or call toll free:
1–800–893–5777.

The University of Alberta Press gratefully acknowl-
edges the support received for its publishing pro-
gram from The Canada Council for the Arts. The
University of Alberta Press also gratefully acknowl-
edges the financial support of the Government of
Canada through the Book Publishing Industry
Development Program (BPIDP) and from the Alberta
Foundation for the Arts for its publishing activities.